TROMBONE   **Book 2**

ACCENT ON ACHIEVEMENT

John O'Reilly

and

Mark Williams

A comprehensive band method that develops creativity and musicianship

Dear Band Student:

Congratulations on completing the first book of **ACCENT ON ACHIEVEMENT**. You have already learned a great deal and are well on your way to becoming an accomplished musician. Book 2 will take you even further on this journey. You will play more great music by composers you've already studied, plus 14 new composers. In addition, you'll play rock, jazz, Latin and ragtime pieces, along with fantastic folk songs from around the world. Practice diligently, and you are sure to do great things in the fascinating world of music.

John O'Reilly

Mark Williams

D1384322

Illustrations: Martin Ledyard

Instrument photos (cover and p.1) are courtesy of Yamaha Corporation of America.

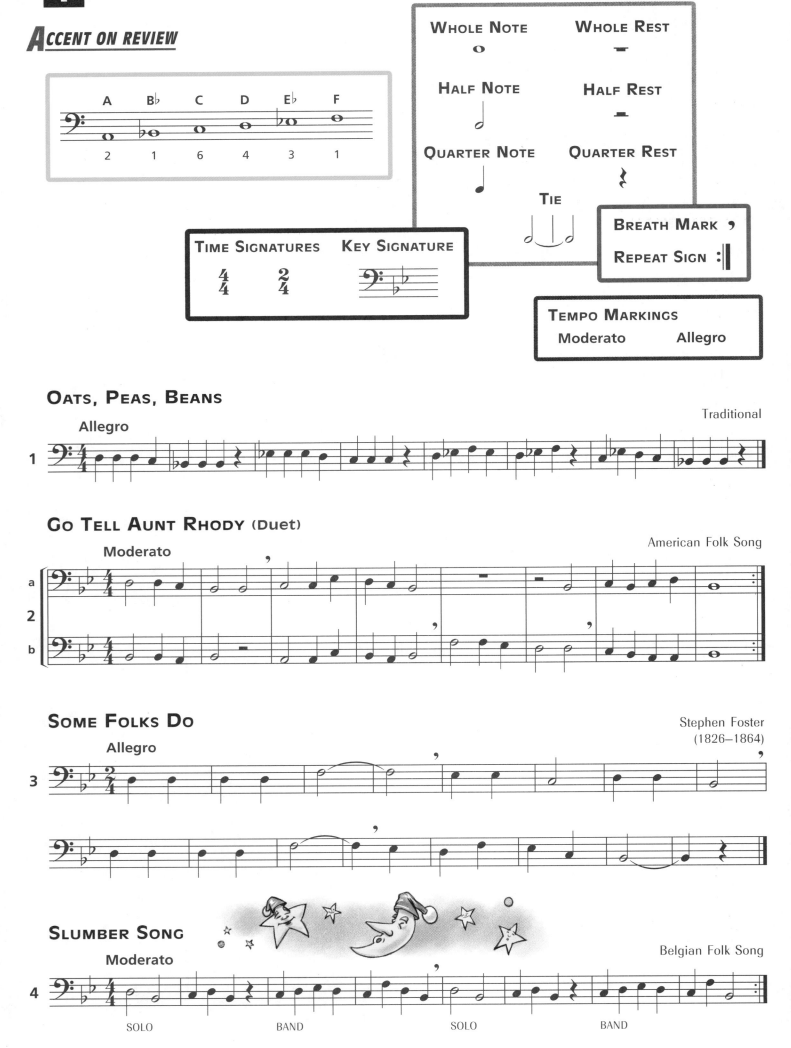

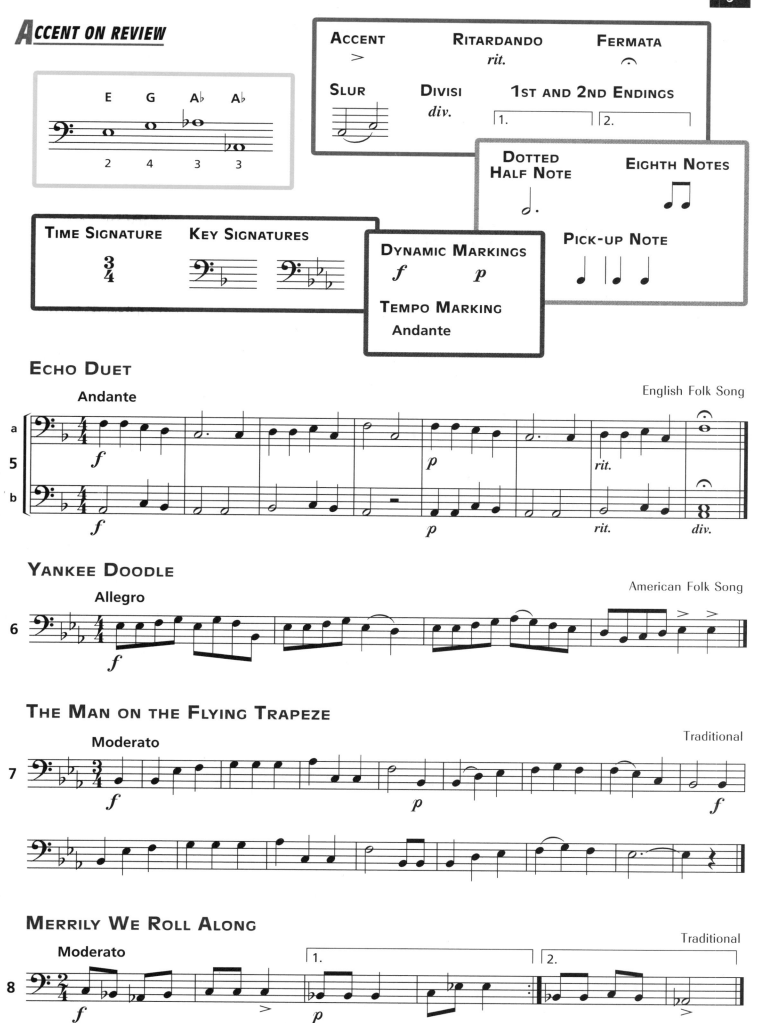

ACCENT ON REVIEW

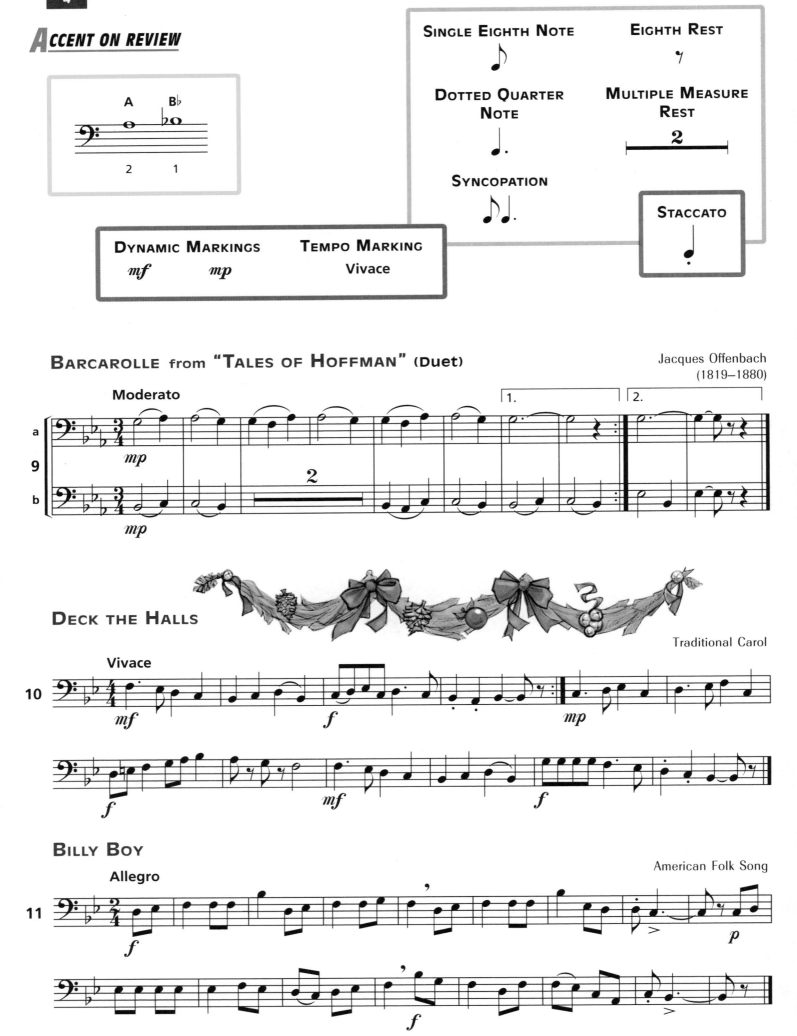

ACCENT ON REVIEW

ACCENT ON PERFORMANCE

MARCH ONWARD

John O'Reilly and Mark Williams

TIME SIGNATURE ¢

Cut Time—same as **2/2**

2/2 = 2 beats in each measure
2/2 = half note receives 1 beat

TEMPO MARKING
Allegretto
Moderately fast tempo

HALF NOTE GETS THE BEAT

Moderato

Count: 1 & 2 & 1 & 2 &

SING NOEL (Round)

Allegretto

Liberian Folk Song

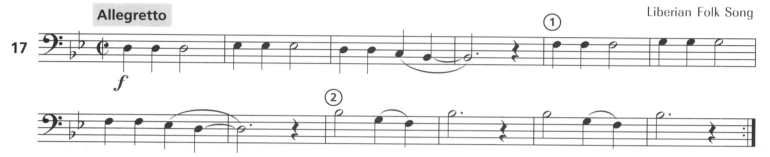

SCARBOROUGH FAIR

Andante

English Folk Song

HIGH SCHOOL CADETS

Allegro

John Philip Sousa
(1854–1932)

ACCENT ON TROMBONE

For more individual technique practice, see page 42, #1.

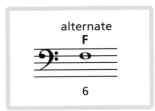

alternate
F
6

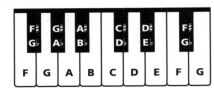

HALF STEP/WHOLE STEP

On a piano keyboard, the distance between any two adjacent keys is called a half step. Two half steps equal one whole step.

A to B♭ = 1/2 step
A to B = whole step
B to C = 1/2 step
B♭ to C = whole step

DIFFERENT STEPS

UP ON THE HOUSETOP

Traditional Carol

ZUM GALI GALI (Duet)

Israeli Folk Song

ACCENT ON THEORY: *Identifying Half Steps and Whole Steps*

Label all half steps with ⌒. Label all whole steps with ⊓.

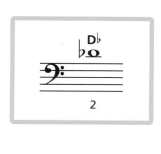

TEMPO MARKING
Maestoso
In a majestic style.

TENUTO

Hold the note for its full value.

A TEMPO

Return to the previous tempo.

STRETCHING HIGHER

Andante

ADVANCE, AUSTRALIA FAIR

Australian National Anthem

DOWN HOME BLUES (Duet)

Allegro

ACCENT ON CREATIVITY: *Free Rhythmic Improvisation*

28 Improvise about eight measures of rhythms using any combination of hand claps, finger snaps and foot stomps. Try to maintain a steady tempo while varying the rhythms and sounds.

SIXTEENTH NOTES

Receive 1/4 beat in $\frac{2}{4}$, $\frac{3}{4}$ and $\frac{4}{4}$ time.

FOUR TO THE BEAT

Moderato

29

Count: 1 e & a 2 & 3 &

THE THUNDERER

John Philip Sousa
(1854–1932)

Allegro

30

HARVEST SONG

Estonian Folk Song

Allegretto

31

SIMPLE GIFTS

American Folk Song

Moderato

32

Fine

D.S. al Fine

ACCENT ON TROMBONE

33

For more individual technique practice, see page 42, #2.

*A*CCENT ON PERFORMANCE

HOLIDAY FANTASY

Arranged by
John O'Reilly and Mark Williams

ACCENT ON CREATIVITY: Passing Tones and Neighbor Tones

Write your own variation on this theme by adding passing tones (notes between pitches a third apart) and neighbor tones (above or below repeated pitches).

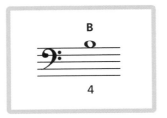

TWO SIXTEENTHS AND AN EIGHTH NOTE

1 e & (a) 2 e & (a)

MORE SIXTEENTHS

Moderato

45

mf

TAFTA HINDI

Arabic Folk Song

Allegretto

46

f-p

f

p

IL EST NÉ

French-Canadian Folk Song

Moderato

47

mp

mf

mp

Fine

D.C. al Fine

mf

f-mf

PAT-A-PAN

French Folk Song

Allegretto

48

mp

mf

ACCENT ON TROMBONE

49

f

For more individual technique practice, see page 42, #3 & 4.

DOTTED EIGHTH NOTE

Receives 3/4 beat in
2/4, 3/4 and 4/4 time.

DOTTED EIGHTHS

Andante

50

mp　　*< mf*　　*> mp*

BRIDAL CHORUS from "LOHENGRIN"

Richard Wagner
(1813–1883)

Maestoso

51

mf　　*< f*　　*> < f*

THEME from "UNFINISHED SYMPHONY"

Franz Schubert
(1797–1828)

Moderato

52

mp

p

ITALIAN STREET SONG

Victor Herbert
(1859–1924)

Allegro

53

f　　*> mp*　　*f*

ACCENT ON THEORY　MAJOR SCALE CONSTRUCTION: All major scales contain the same pattern of whole steps and half steps. Study this pattern in the example below. Now build your own major scale beginning on the note given, adding any sharps or flats as necessary. Note names must be in alphabetical order.

whole step | whole step | half step | whole step | whole step | whole step | half step

54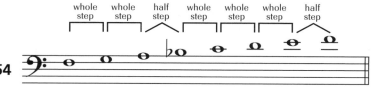

ACCENT ON PERFORMANCE

CYBERSPACE OVERTURE

John O'Reilly and Mark Williams

LOOKING SHARP

O CANADA

Canadian National Anthem

ARIA from "THE MARRIAGE OF FIGARO"

Wolfgang A. Mozart
(1756–1791)

ACCENT ON CREATIVITY: *Improvisation on Chord Changes*

Improvise your own melody using the notes contained in each triad (three-note chord).
You may also use passing or neighbor tones as long as they are of short duration.

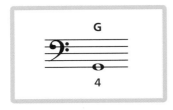

D.C. (DA CAPO) AL CODA

Go back to the beginning;
then skip to the coda.

RANGE BUILDER

Moderato

59

mf

FLOWER DRUM SONG

Chinese Folk Song

Andante

60

mp

mf   *mp*

6——   6——

NU ÄR DET JUL IGEN

Swedish Folk Song

Moderato

61

mf

COLONEL BOGEY

Kenneth Alford
(1881–1945)

Allegro

To Coda ⊕

62

f

D.C. al Coda   ⊕ *Coda*

ACCENT ON TROMBONE

63

6   6

mf

For more individual technique practice, see page 42, #5 and page 43, #6.

ENHARMONICS

Any two notes that are written differently, but sound the same.

C# = D♭
F# = G♭
B = C♭

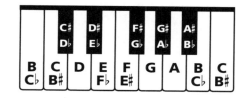

CHROMATIC CRAWL

Moderato

THEME from "PIANO CONCERTO NO. 2"

Sergei Rachmaninoff (1873–1943)

Andante

IN THE HALL OF THE MOUNTAIN KING

Edvard Grieg (1843–1907)

Moderato

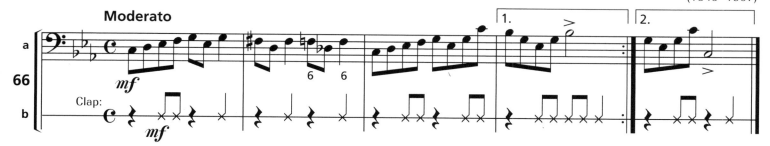

OVERTURE from "THE BARBER OF SEVILLE"

Gioacchino Rossini (1792–1868)

Vivace

ACCENT ON THEORY

Rewrite each of these notes as its enharmonic equivalent.

> **TIME SIGNATURE**
>
> **3** = 3 beats in each measure
> **8** = eighth note receives 1 beat

EIGHTH NOTE GETS THE BEAT

Moderato

69   *mf*

Count: 1 2 3

TARANTELLA (Duet)

Italian Folk Song

Allegro

70

f

f

mp

mp

BATTLE HYMN OF THE REPUBLIC

Traditional

Maestoso

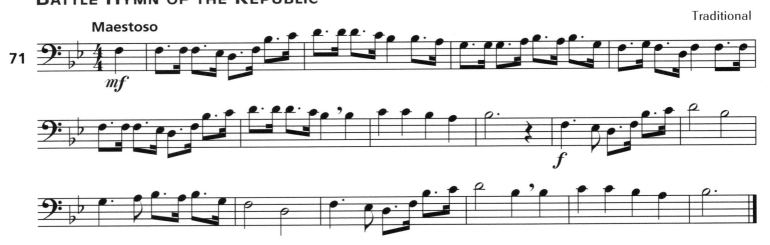

71   *mf*

f

ACCENT ON CREATIVITY: *Composition Based on a Rhythmic Pattern*

Write your own short composition, using the rhythmic pattern ♪♪♩ in different ways.
Be sure to include: 1) clef sign 2) key signature 3) time signature.   Play your composition.

72

ACCENT ON PERFORMANCE

WATER MUSIC

George F. Handel (1685–1759)
Arr. by John O'Reilly and Mark Williams

TIME SIGNATURE

6 = 6 beats in each measure
8 = eighth note receives 1 beat

D.S. (DAL SEGNO) AL CODA

Go back to the sign 𝄋;
then skip to the coda.

SIX TO THE BAR

ROW, ROW, ROW YOUR BOAT (Round)

American Folk Song

I'S THE B'Y (Duet)

Canadian Folk Song
(Newfoundland)

THE ENTERTAINER

Scott Joplin
(1868–1917)

To Coda ⊕

D.S. al Coda

⊕ *Coda*

ACCENT ON TROMBONE

For more individual technique practice, see page 43, #7.

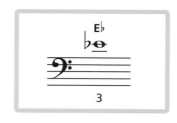

TEMPO MARKING
Andantino
Slightly faster than Andante.

STILL HIGHER

CALYPSO CLIMB (Duet)

I SAW THREE SHIPS

Traditional Carol

THE STAR-SPANGLED BANNER

U.S. National Anthem

ACCENT ON THEORY Rewrite the following example in cut time.

24

MOLTO RIT.

Dramatically slow down the tempo.

SMOOTH SLURRING

HABAÑERA from "CARMEN"

Georges Bizet
(1838–1875)

YODELING SONG

Austrian Folk Song

THEME from "VIOLIN CONCERTO IN D"

Ludwig van Beethoven
(1770–1827)

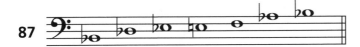 CCENT ON CREATIVITY: Improvisation on a Blues Scale

Using the pitches shown, improvise your own melody using any rhythms you know.
You may play these notes in any order, repeat notes, or use rests.

CLOG DANCE

Moderato

HOPAK from "THE FAIR AT SOROCHINSK"

Modest Mussorgsky
(1839–1881)

Allegretto

O TANNENBAUM

German Folk Song

BLOW AWAY THE MORNING DEW

English Folk Song

Allegro

ACCENT ON TROMBONE

For more individual technique practice, see page 43, #8.

ACCENT ON PERFORMANCE

FIESTA MEXICALI

John O'Reilly and Mark Williams

DYNAMIC MARKINGS

pp   *ff*

Pianissimo—very soft   Fortissimo—very loud

BEAMING OVER A REST

BEAM ME UP

THE SORCERER'S APPRENTICE

Paul Dukas
(1865–1935)

COUNTRY GARDENS (Duet)

English Folk Song

ACCENT ON THEORY

Draw the correct bar lines, then write in the counting and clap.

ACCENT ON CREATIVITY: Extended Composition

101 Write your own composition of any length, using a separate sheet of music paper. Use some repeated rhythmic and/or melodic patterns to create unity. Use some contrasting material to create variety. Play your composition.

EIGHTH NOTE TRIPLETS

1 trip-let 2 trip-let

GRACE NOTE

A quick note, usually played just before the beat.

THREE TO THE BEAT

Moderato

102

mf

1. 2.

TRIPLET SONG

Andantino

French Folk Song

103

mp

p

mf

FINALE from "NEW WORLD SYMPHONY"

Allegro

Antonin Dvořák
(1841–1904)

104

ff

Fine

D.C. al Fine

mf

PROCESSION OF THE NOBLES

Maestoso

Nicolai Rimsky-Korsakov
(1844–1908)

105

f

ff

*A*CCENT ON TROMBONE

106

f

For more individual technique practice, see page 43, #9.

THE OUTER LIMITS

107 Moderato

NOW IS THE MONTH OF MAYING (Duet)

Thomas Morley
(1559–1602)

108 Allegretto

a

b

LA DONNA É MOBILE

Giuseppe Verdi
(1813–1901)

109 Moderato

SOLDIER'S CHORUS from "FAUST"

Charles Gounod
(1818–1893)

110 Moderato

MARCH from "NUTCRACKER"

Peter Ilyich Tchaikovsky
(1840–1893)

111 Allegro

For more individual technique practice, see page 43, #10.

ACCENT ON PERFORMANCE

SOUSA ON PARADE

John Philip Sousa
(1854–1932)
Arr. by John O'Reilly
and Mark Williams

TROMBONE SOLO

WHEN JOHNNY COMES MARCHING HOME

Arr. by John O'Reilly and Mark Williams

ACCENT ON ENSEMBLES

JAZZ FOR A SATURDAY AFTERNOON

John O'Reilly and Mark Williams

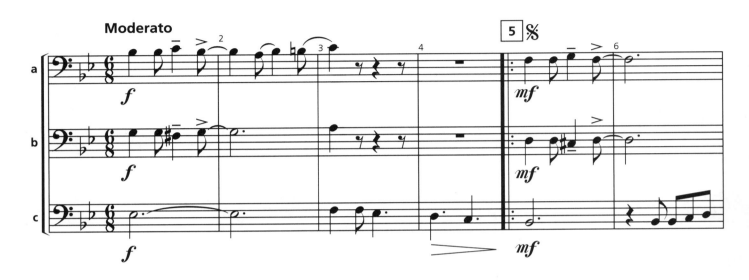

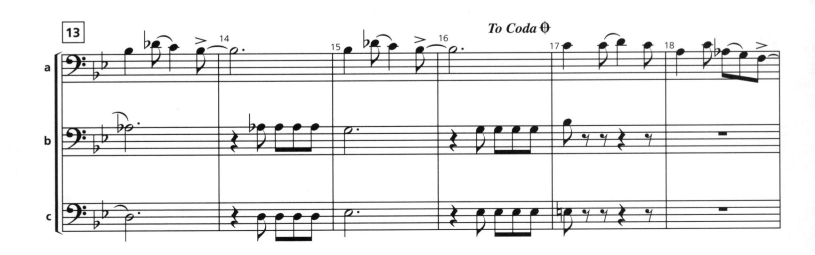

ACCENT ON SCALES

Bb MAJOR SCALE (Concert Bb)

G HARMONIC MINOR SCALE (Concert G)

G MELODIC MINOR SCALE (Concert G)

F MAJOR SCALE (Concert F)

D HARMONIC MINOR SCALE (Concert D)

D MELODIC MINOR SCALE (Concert D)

Eb MAJOR SCALE (Concert Eb)

C HARMONIC MINOR SCALE (Concert C)

C MELODIC MINOR SCALE (Concert C)

A♭ Major Scale (Concert A♭)

F Harmonic Minor Scale (Concert F)

F Melodic Minor Scale (Concert F)

C Major Scale (Concert C)

A Harmonic Minor Scale (Concert A)

A Melodic Minor Scale (Concert A)

D♭ Major Scale (Concert D♭)

B♭ Harmonic Minor Scale (Concert B♭)

B♭ Melodic Minor Scale (Concert B♭)

Chromatic Scale (Trombones only)

ACCENT ON RHYTHMS

ACCENT ON RESTS

ACCENT ON TROMBONE

ACCENT ON CHORALES

WE GATHER TOGETHER
Netherlands Folk Song

NOW THANK WE ALL OUR GOD
Johann Sebastian Bach
(1685–1750)

MA-OZ TSUR (ROCK OF AGES)
Traditional Hanukkah Song

ALL THROUGH THE NIGHT
Welsh Folk Song

ETERNAL FATHER, STRONG TO SAVE
Navy Hymn

GLOSSARY

ACCENT (>) Play the note stronger

ADAGIO Slightly slower than Andante

ALFORD, KENNETH English composer (1881–1945)

ALLEGRETTO Moderately fast tempo

ALLEGRO Fast tempo

ANDANTE Moderately slow tempo

ANDANTINO Slightly faster than Andante

A TEMPO Return to the previous tempo

BACH, JOHANN SEBASTIAN German composer (1685–1750)

BEETHOVEN, LUDWIG VAN German composer (1770–1827)

BIZET, GEORGES French composer (1838–1875)

COMMON TIME (C) Same as $\frac{4}{4}$ time signature

CUT TIME (¢) Same as $\frac{2}{2}$ time signature

CRESCENDO (⎯⎯◁) Get louder gradually

D.C. (DA CAPO) AL CODA Go back to the beginning; then skip to the coda

D.C. (DA CAPO) AL FINE Go back to the beginning and play until Fine

DIMINUENDO (▷⎯⎯) Get softer gradually

D.S. (DAL SEGNO) AL CODA Go back to the sign 𝄋; then skip to the coda

D.S. (DAL SEGNO) AL FINE Go back to the sign 𝄋 and play until Fine

DUKAS, PAUL French composer (1865–1935)

DVOŘÁK, ANTONIN Czech composer (1841–1904)

ENHARMONICS Any two notes that are written differently, but sound the same. (F♯ = G♭)

FERMATA (⌢) Hold the note longer

FLAT (♭) Lowers the pitch of a note one half step

FORTE (f) Loud

f–p Play loud the first time and soft the second time

FORTISSIMO (ff) Very loud

FOSTER, STEPHEN American composer (1826–1864)

GOUNOD, CHARLES French composer (1818–1893)

GRACE NOTE A quick note, usually played just before the beat

GRIEG, EDVARD Norwegian composer (1843–1907)

HALF STEP The distance between any two adjacent keys on the piano

HANDEL, GEORGE F. English composer of German birth (1685–1759)

HERBERT, VICTOR American composer (1859–1924)

JOPLIN, SCOTT American composer (1868–1917)

KEY SIGNATURE Indicates notes which are to be flatted or sharped throughout

LARGO Very slow

MAESTOSO In a majestic style

MEZZO FORTE (mf) Medium loud

MEZZO PIANO (mp) Medium soft

MENDELSSOHN, FELIX German composer (1809–1847)

MODERATO Medium tempo

MOLTO RIT. Dramatically slow down the tempo

MORLEY, THOMAS English composer (1559–1602)

MOZART, WOLFGANG A. Austrian composer (1756–1791)

MUSSORGSKY, MODEST Russian composer (1839–1881)

NATURAL (♮) Cancels a flat or sharp until the next bar line

OFFENBACH, JACQUES French composer (1819–1880)

PIANISSIMO (pp) Very soft

PIANO (p) Soft

RACHMANINOFF, SERGEI Russian composer (1873–1943)

RIMSKY-KORSAKOV, NICOLAI Russian composer (1844–1908)

RITARDANDO (RIT.) Gradually slow down the tempo

ROSSINI, GIOACCHINO Italian composer (1792–1868)

SHARP (♯) Raises the pitch of a note one half step

SCHUBERT, FRANZ German composer (1797–1828)

SFORZANDO (sfz) A strong accent

SOUSA, JOHN PHILIP American composer (1854–1932)

STACCATO (·) Play the note ½ its normal length

TCHAIKOVSKY, PETER I. Russian composer (1840–1893)

TENUTO (–) Hold the note for its full value

TRANSPOSING Rewriting a melody, beginning on a different starting pitch.

VERDI, GIUSEPPE Italian composer (1813–1901)

VIVACE Very fast tempo

VIVALDI, ANTONIO Italian composer (1678–1741)

WAGNER, RICHARD German composer (1813–1883)

WHOLE STEP Two half steps

TROMBONE POSITION CHART

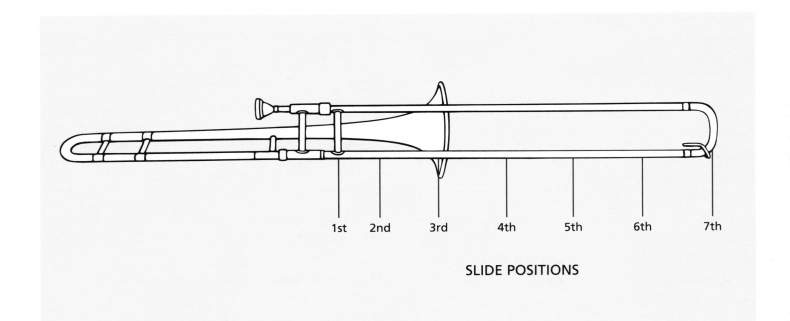

1st   2nd   3rd   4th   5th   6th   7th

SLIDE POSITIONS

Numbers under notes indicate slide positions.

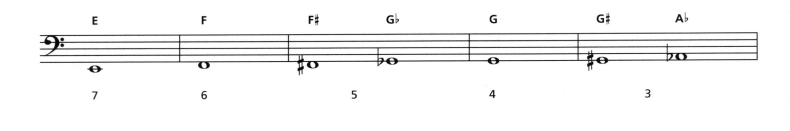

E	F	F#	Gb	G	G#	Ab
7	6	5		4	3	

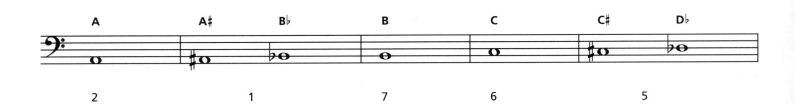

A	A#	Bb	B	C	C#	Db
2	1		7	6	5	

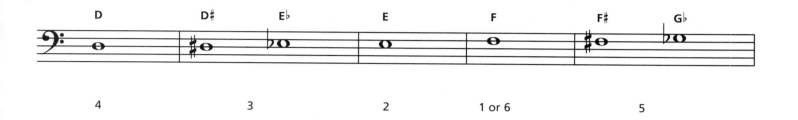

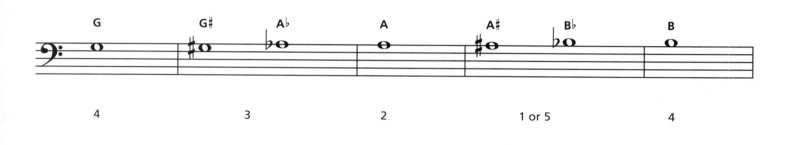

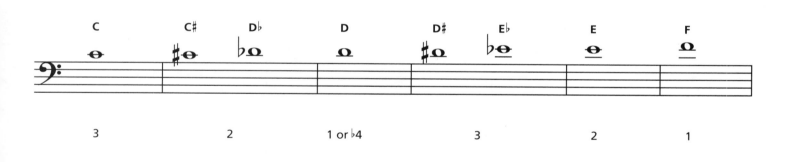

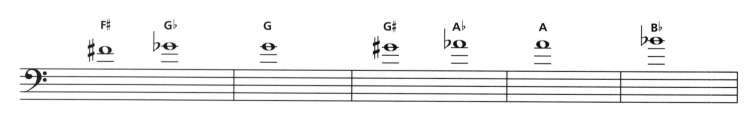

HOME PRACTICE RECORD

Week	Date	ASSIGNMENT	Mon	Tue	Wed	Thur	Fri	Sat	Sun	Total	Parent Signature
1											
2											
3											
4											
5											
6											
7											
8											
9											
10											
11											
12											
13											
14											
15											
16											
17											
18											
19											
20											
21											
22											
23											
24											
25											
26											
27											
28											
29											
30											
31											
32											
33											
34											
35											
36											